The Theatre of the Soul
A Monodrama in One Act

N. N. Evreinov

Translator: Marie Potapenko

Christopher St. John

Alpha Editions

This edition published in 2020

ISBN : 9789354186653 (Hardback)

ISBN : 9789354189647 (Paperback)

Design and Setting By
Alpha Editions
www.alphaedis.com
email - alphaedis@gmail.com

As per information held with us this book is in Public Domain.
This book is a reproduction of an important historical work. Alpha Editions uses the best technology to reproduce historical work in the same manner it was first published to preserve its original nature. Any marks or number seen are left intentionally to preserve its true form.

Cast at The Little Theatre, March 8th, 1915.

The Professor	MICHAEL SHERBROOKE.
M1 (Rational Entity of the Soul)	A. B. TAPPING.
M2 (Emotional Entity) . . .	CAMPBELL GULLAN.
M3 (Subliminal Entity) . .	K. MAUNSELL.
1st Concept of the Dancer . .	MARGARET MORRIS.
2nd Concept of the Dancer . .	L. WALSH-HALL.
1st Concept of the Wife . . .	
2nd Concept of the Wife . .	MARY ROSS SHORE.
The Porter	CHARLES GOODHART.

Produced by Miss Edith Craig.

Cast announced to play at The Alhambra, November 18th, 1915.

The Professor	MICHAEL SHERBROOKE.
M1 (Rational Entity of the Soul)	FISHER WHITE.
M2 (Emotional Entity) . . .	CAMPBELL GULLAN.
M3 (Subliminal Entity) . .	KENNETH KENT.
1st Concept of the Dancer . .	ETHEL LEVEY.
2nd Concept of the Dancer . .	ELEANOR ELDER.
1st Concept of the Wife . .	LILIAN BRAITHWAITE.
2nd Concept of the Wife . .	ESMÉ HUBBARD.
The Porter	GIRTON BARRIE.

FOREWORD
BY
CHRISTOPHER ST. JOHN

I SHOULD like to be able to preface " The Theatre of the Soul " with some account of the author Nikolai Evréinof, but I have to confess that I know too little of him, and his work, to do him justice. What I do know is that he has a considerable reputation in Russia as a daring and unconventional dramatist who has also distinguished himself by interesting experiments in the production of plays. Evréinof is still very young, and thinks, with a modesty rare in the young, that he is a beginner in the dramatist's art, but he has achieved enough to create both admiration and envy. One compatriot of his tells me that he is a mere *poseur*; another that he is more profound than any other living Russian dramatist for all his assumption of levity. In style, so far as Evréinof recalls any one, he recalls Tchekof, the Tchekof, that is to say, of such farces as " The Wedding " and " The Jubilee." But these famous little plays taste rather like sweet lemonade (indubitably made of real lemons) after one has drunk a little of Evréinof's strong essential life.

Evréinof is connected with the Parody Theatre in Petrograd. There he produced Shaw's " Candida," with a black boy reading the stage directions, which Evréinof considers the most brilliant part of the play, and there he gave the first act of Gogol's "Inspector-General" several times in one evening in the different styles of modern stage production—after the Art Theatre, Moscow, after Gordon Craig, and so on. In this satirical venture Evréinof was hitting out at the cranks who want to reform the theatre or make a new thing which shall be more artistic than the theatre. For Evréinof holds that the theatre exists, and cannot be altered, although it can be used as a means of expression. He thinks that the word "theatrical" ought not to be a term of reproach, and has written a book on the subject entitled "The Theatre—as Such." He is in the position of being a rebel against the rebels, and is no more in sympathy with the Art Theatre, Moscow, and all similar enterprises than with the ordinary commercial theatre.

Horace's "ridendo dicere severum" would appear to be Evréinof's motto. Even in "The Theatre of the Soul" I feel that he is being profound—with his tongue in his cheek. Many critics after the first production of the play in England criticised its "crude psychology"; but Evréinof may be right in his assumption that the reflections of the soul *are* crude. Every one who thinks at all knows that the interior of a human soul has very little furniture, and that what takes place there is astonishingly simple. What a man expresses through the medium of his brain and personality is complicated, both in its beauty and its ugliness, but the thing from which this elaboration of thought and action is evolved is as it exists in the soul elemental whether the soul be a philosopher's or a peasant's. For this reason it seems to me that the crudeness of "The Theatre of the Soul" is a virtue rather than a defect.

It may be as well to give here a straightforward account of the circumstances in which " The Theatre of the Soul " came to be included in the programme of the matinée at the Alhambra on November 18th, from which, as the public still remember, it was removed at the last moment in a manner insulting alike to the author, the producer, and the actors and actresses who were ready to interpret it.

In the spring of this year I brought the English version which I had made with the assistance of Madame Marie Potapenko to the notice of the Pioneer Players and it was produced at the Little Theatre by Miss Edith Craig on March 8th. It was received with indisputable enthusiasm by an audience fairly representative of the best elements in that mysterious entity " the Public," and provoked the critics to express both admiration and censure with more energy than they usually display. To Mr. William Archer it seemed " extremely original and striking," to Mr. E. F. Spence " a weird clever piece," to another critic " poor and puerile and portentous." The thing worth remembering in this connection is that there was no suggestion whatever in the Press that the play was one which ought never to have been brought on to the loftily moral English stage.

In October a distinguished lady on the Committee of the Pioneer Players suggested to Lady Paget, the organiser of the matinée on " Russia's Day," that she should invite the society to repeat Evréinof's play at the Alhambra. The invitation was accepted, and Miss Edith Craig collected a splendid cast, rehearsed indefatigably, and did her best to overcome the many difficulties which confront any one who tries to give a finished performance at one of these monster charity matinées. Not long before it was to take place I was asked for a copy of the play to send to the Lord Chamberlain, as it had not been licensed. That some one was at work even then trying to prevent the performance became clear to me later. The business manager for the matinée came to see me and told me that it was no use sending the play—as the Censor would not pass it. It was not fit for the Alhambra audience. This I could not deny, as there is neither inanity nor nudity in "The Theatre of the Soul," but I could, and did, argue that an audience gathered together at the Alhambra on "Russia's Day" would not be an Alhambra audience —that presumably there would be people present in the theatre with some interest in Russia who might prefer a play by a Russian dramatist to jokes about Charlie Chaplin, and a *ballet décolleté* and *rétroussé*. At any rate I preferred an official decision as to the fitness of "The Theatre of the Soul" for public performance to an unofficial one, and insisted that a licence should be applied for.

That it was granted was evidently a disappointment to Mr. Charlot, the manager of the Alhambra, who for some reason disapproved of the play. After he had watched the dress rehearsal which took place on the Alhambra stage on the morning of the proposed performance, he sent an abrupt message to Miss Craig to inform her that the play was not to be done. No reason was given, no apology offered, no regret expressed to any one concerned in the production.

It was natural to think that there must be a weighty reason for this summary withdrawal of a Russian play from a programme designed as a compliment to

Russia. Evréinof, the author, Miss Craig, to whom fell the privilege of first producing one of his plays here, and myself, were all entitled to the courtesy of an explanation. We can hardly swallow the one conveyed to us indirectly, that it was the repulsive incident of a woman's wig being taken off and her bald head displayed, which made Mr. Charlot withdraw the play ! Bald heads are often seen at the Alhambra and are not considered repulsive in the first row of stalls. And in that " family " play, David Garrick, the hero snatches off a lady's wig.

It is an incident like this which makes England the derision of artists all the world over. On the very day that the newspapers were printing columns of gush about Russia's art and boasting of English sympathy with it, a Russian dramatist's work is declared unfit for the stage of a London music hall, and the public are left to draw the inference that it is indelicate and obscene, as no courageous avowal is made of the true reason for conduct both stupid and ill-bred.

In the production of the play Miss Edith Craig used a queer and fascinating machinery, of the simplest kind, by which little was seen of the three entities of the soul beyond their faces appearing at different levels out of intense darkness. The heart was represented by a glowing red space which appeared to pulsate owing to an effect of light. The concepts of the women were seen in the foreground and were brilliantly lighted. The whole effect was thrilling and beautiful, and helped enormously to create a dramatic atmosphere.

The Pioneer Players are going to do more of Evréinof's work, but in future they will try to protect it from the insult of people not on a level with it.

THE THEATRE OF THE SOUL

A MONODRAMA IN ONE ACT

CHARACTERS

THE PROFESSOR.
M1, The Rational Entity of the Soul.
M2, The Emotional Entity.
M3, The Subliminal Entity.
M1's CONCEPT OF THE WIFE.
M2's CONCEPT OF THE WIFE.
M1's CONCEPT OF THE DANCER.
M2's CONCEPT OF THE DANCER.
THE PORTER.

The action passes in the soul in the period of half a second.

The prologue takes place before the curtain. A blackboard. Chalks.

The PROFESSOR *enters from the wings, stops before the blackboard, and after having bowed to the audience, takes his chalk and begins his demonstration.*

PROFESSOR. Ladies and Gentlemen,—When the unknown author of " The Theatre of the Soul," the play that is going to be presented to you this evening, came to me some weeks ago with the manuscript, I confess that the title of his work did not inspire me with much confidence. " Here," I thought, " is another of the many little sensational plays with which the theatre is deluged." I was all the more agreeably surprised to gather from this first reading that "The Theatre of the Soul" is a genuinely scientific work, in every respect abreast with the latest developments in psychophysiology. As you know, the researches of Wundt, Freud, Theophile Ribot and others have proved in the most conclusive way that the human soul is not indivisible, but on the contrary is composed of several selfs, the natures of which are different. Thus if M represents I myself (*He writes on the board.*)

$$M = M1 + M2 + M3 \ldots Mn.$$

Fichte lays down the principle that if M is the "entity self," the world is not M. That is lucidity itself, gentlemen! According to the dicta of modern science, however, if the world is not "M," neither is the entity self. This is quite clear, is it not, gentlemen? Thus I, myself or M—is not a simple quantity, because it comprises several entities. I have come to the conclusion that there are three entities, M1, M2, M3. M1 is the rational self—the REASON, if you prefer to call it so. M2 is the emotional self, or, as we may call it, FEELING. M3 is the psychical self, or the ETERNAL. This is easy to understand, I think. These three "M's" or "selfs" constitute the great integral self.

(*He writes:* "M1 + M2 + M3 = M, *the entire personality.*")

You will ask me now, perhaps, where the component elements, of which the complete personality is composed, are situated. The ancients believed that they were situated in the liver, but the author of the work which is to be presented to you holds, and with far better reason I think, that the human soul manifests itself in that part of the physical breast which a man instinctively strikes when he wishes to emphasise his good faith, or even when he uses such expressions as "I am distressed to the soul," or "I rejoice with my whole soul," or "My soul burns with indignation." Consequently the scene of the human soul appears to us like this :

(He draws a plan on the board with different coloured chalks and proceeds to explain it.)

This plan, ladies and gentlemen, represents, as no doubt you can see, a large heart, with the beginning of its main red artery. It makes from 55 to 125 pulsations a minute, and lies between the two lungs which fill and empty themselves from fourteen to eighteen times a minute. Here you see a little system of nerves, threads of nerves, pale in colour, and constantly agitated by vibration which we will compare with a telephone. Such is the scene in which the "entity self" plays its part. But, ladies and gentlemen, science does not confine itself to explaining things. It also offers us consolation. For instance, it is not enough to say, "I've done a foolish thing." One ought to know which of the three entities is responsible. If it is M2, or the emotional self, no great harm is done. If it is the psychical entity, the matter need not be taken very seriously either. But if it be the rational self it is time to be alarmed. At this point, ladies and gentlemen, I feel myself under the necessity of suspending my explanations, and of giving way to the author, to the artists, and to you, ladies and gentlemen, who I know will prove yourselves worthy critics of this admirable little work.

(The PROFESSOR *retires.)*

The board is removed. The curtain goes up, and the interior of the human soul is seen, as it has been described by the PROFESSOR. *On the scene, that is to say on the Diaphragm, the three entities, who bear a close resemblance to each other, are discovered. All three are dressed in black, but their costumes differ.* M1 *wears a frock-coat.* M2 *an artist's blouse and a red tie.* M3 *a well-worn travelling dress. The other differences between the three entities are indicated as follows :* M1 *is a person who wears spectacles and has a quiet, sober manner, his hair is slightly grey and carefully brushed. His lips are thin.* M2 *has a very youthful manner. His gestures and movements are quick, lively and a little exaggerated. His hair is untidy, his lips are full and red.* M3 *wears a black mask. He slumbers in the foreground, his bag under his arm, in the attitude of a traveller, worn out by fatigue.*

M2. (*At the telephone.*) Hullo ! What ? You can't hear me ? I am speaking loud enough ! What ? It makes your ear vibrate ? That is because your nerves are overstrained. Now listen. Brandy ! Do you hear ? Brandy !

M1. Don't forget that it is you who are forcing him to drink a third bottle for no reason except that you want to pass the time somehow. Poor heart ! Look how it is beating !

M2. You would prefer it to be always in a state of stupor, like the sub-conscious ! A charming sort of existence !

M1. If the heart goes on beating like that, it will not be for long.

M2. Well, what does that matter? Sooner or later it must stop.

M1. Now you are quoting my exact words.

M2. And why not? You sometimes talk sense.

M1. Please don't touch the nerves. You have been told already that——

(*Each time that the nerves are touched, a low jingling sound is heard.*)

M2. (*With anger.*) Told me! Who has told me? And by what right? Who the devil dares order me about as if I were a servant? I am a poet. Love, passion, that is I! Without me, what would there be here but dust and mildew . . . a museum, a cemetery? . . . Everything is nothing—without passion.

M1. You talk like a fool.

M2. It's the absolute truth. Whose fault is it if we drink?

M1. It is not you, of course, who are always crying out for brandy.

M2. And if I do, isn't it forced on me? Isn't it because in your society there is nothing for our poor being to do but hang himself?

M1. Come now! You know very well that it is you, not I, who are the cause of all his misfortunes. Yes, you, the emotional self. What are you but a selfish libertine, a wreck of a man? Have you ever had any taste for study, ever taken any interest in noble, intellectual work, ever reflected on the idea of moral dignity?

M2. You are nothing but a pedant, a wretched academic dry-as-dust.

M1. Yet I despise you, O emotional self.
M2. And I despise you as much, O rational entity.
(*He passes his hand over the nerves with a big sweeping movement.*)
M1. Stop that. You shall not touch *my* nerves.
M2. By what right do you interfere ? Allow me to remind you that we possess these nerves in common, and that when I touch them it is my nerves which become on edge as well as yours ! When, thanks to you, my nerves are numbed, I become as stupid as an ox . . . as stupid, that is to say, as *you*. You shall not prevent my touching them. I like them taut and strained. Then they become like Apollo's lute, and on them I can play the hymn to love and liberty ! (*He plays on the nerves. The heart begins to beat more strongly. Speaking at the telephone.*) Brandy !
M1. (*Snatching away the telephone.*) Valerian !
M2. (*Snatching away the telephone.*) Brandy !
M1. (*Again possessing himself of it.*) Valerian—do you hear ? What ? There is none left ? Then go to the chemist's. Valerian—30 drops in a glass of water. (*He leaves the telephone. The two entities walk up and down. They meet.*) Are you calm now ?
M2. What are you ?
M1. You can see for yourself.
(*They both approach the subconscious entity. A silence.*)
M2. What is he ?
M1. Supremely quiescent, as always. Don't disturb his peace. If you do, it is you who will suffer for it. (*At the telephone.*) Have you taken your drops ? Good. I will try and make him listen to reason. But the fact is, I don't grasp the principal point. This

woman has attracted you by the originality of her talent, and if, in addition, she has—Very well! But for that to abandon wife and children . . . excuse me, it is not a solution. At least, unless we are to embrace polygamy . . . the ideal of a savage, more capable of appreciating the curve of a leg and the line of a back than the wondrous architecture of an immortal temple —I mean the soul.'. . .

M2. Oh! what do all your opinions and beliefs matter to me? She is beautiful. What's the use of reasoning?

M1. The brute beast doesn't reason certainly, but man—to whom the logic of feeling should be familiar— (*To the telephone as he passes.*)

M2. Good heavens! How dull, how insensible you are . . . and what anguish I endure from being bound to so colourless, so insipid a companion. . . .

M1. You used not to talk like this.

M2. You're right there. I even loved you when we worked together harmoniously I shall never forget the service you rendered me when I was consumed with love for Annette! To get the better of that very cautious young woman, and to cheat the vigilance of her parents—that was—Oh, on that occasion you showed no lack of cleverness! But of late you have become not merely less intelligent, but as dull as a rusty razor.

M1. Thank you for the compliment! I am not sensitive. Also I am aware that brandy has something to do with your opinion of me.

M2. Oh, God, how beautiful she is! You must have forgotten how beautiful, how gay! Yes, I know she is only a café chantant singer—but what of that?

You can't remember her face, her figure . . . her whole lovely personality. . . . I will show her to you. (*He summons up from the left the seductive concept of the singer.*) Sing as you sang yesterday, beloved beautiful one. As you sang yesterday, the day before yesterday, a week ago, last Sunday. Sing, I beg you. (*To M1, who has turned his back on the woman's image.*) Oh! why don't you help me ?

  (*The first concept of the singer. She sings and dances to the rhythm of the heart which beats joyously.*)

Is it you ?
Is it you ?
Are you the nice young fellow
Who the other day was near me—
So near me in the darkness of the train ?
I could not see you then,
For it was much too dark,
But I should like to know.
Is it you ?
Is it you
Whom my kisses so sweet
Made so madly in love ?

In the train the other day
A gentleman sat near me.
I turned my head to look at him
But at that very moment
The light went out.
Into my arms then my maddened neighbour throws
 himself,
I kiss him ardently, embrace him, but since that day
Vainly I have searched for him.

Longing, I say to every man I see,
"Is it you?
Is it you?
Are you the nice young fellow
Who the other day was near me—
So near me in the darkness of the train?"

M2. (*Enchanted.*) Oh, rapture! The whole universe is not worth such joy! Those legs, those feet! Dear God, what carpet in the wide world is fit for the touch of those lovely feet, so lovely that they make me weep?... Dance on me! Dance in me! Swing to and fro, angelic censer! (*He embraces her feet, her hands.*)

M1. What lunacy—what folly! Leave her! It is all imagination. She is not like that. You kiss a painted face, you caress false hair. She is forty if she's a day. Leave her! All that you see and feel is false. See her as she is, see *reality!* (*At the beginning of his speech, the first concept of the woman vanishes R. whence M1 summons the second concept of the singer, ludicrously aged and deformed.*) Look! Look, if you would know the truth. Look at the divine feet—hard and coarse! Look at the exquisite head! *Tête de veau au naturel* ... without the wig and the curls. (*He lifts off the wig and displays an almost bald head.*) Take out those star-like teeth! (*She takes out her plate.*) Now sing!

(*She sings out of tune, with a nasal twang, and executes some steps with the grace of an old hack being led to the shambles.*)

M2. No, no, this is not reality. This is not the truth! (*To the second concept.*) Go away! Get out of this! (*He pushes her out with violence.*)

M1. Ah! you are angry. Then you acknowledge you are wrong.

M2. I acknowledge nothing of the kind. You have played some trick on me—you——

M1. You know quite well that the creature on whom you are pouring out this mad passion is not worthy to unloose the shoe-strings of the woman whom you are going to deceive and betray. And why? I ask you why? (*He summons from the R. the first concept of the wife, who is nursing a child.*) Because she has always been gentle and kind to you? Because she has nursed your child? Her singing is not that of the café chantant, I know, but listen! Listen to the lullaby that she is crooning to your little one—that is, if your ear is not now too gross to hear a sound so pure. Her voice is tired, you say. Ah! she has been singing for three long nights—nights that she has passed without sleep, waiting, hoping, despairing, aching for you to come home. (*The first concept of the wife sings the lullaby in a low voice.*)

    Sleep, my little one, sleep;
    The pain will soon go, my love.
    Be patient, what did'st thou say?
    "Daddy! Where is my daddy?"
    Daddy will come to thee soon;
    Daddy works hard, my darling,
    But soon he will come with a toy,
    A beautiful toy for thee!
    A wooden horse, would'st thou like?
    Gee-up, gee-up, a horse to ride.
    Good Daddy, kind Daddy—gee-up!
    Sleep, my little one, sleep!

M2. (*Roughly.*) I've had enough of this silly farce.

There is no truth in it. It's a got-up affair. It's all vulgar sentimentality. (*He violently pushes away the first concept of the wife.*) Go away from here, you heroine of melodrama. . . . She is not what you pretend. I know her too well. She has poisoned my whole life. There is no poetry in her, no joy, no passion. She is prose itself, the baldest, the most banal prose, in spite of her heroic attitudes! The eternal housemaid—that's what she is.

> (*He summons the second concept of the wife—a very ordinary and slovenly bourgeoise. Her untidy hair is done in an unbecoming knot. She wears a dirty dressing-gown, stained with coffee, and open at the breast.*)

2ND CONCEPT OF THE WIFE. (*Violently.*) This is a nice business! If my parents only knew the life I lead with this low brute. What surprises me is that he hasn't got the sack from the office long ago—a drunkard like him! Without that cursed brandy he wouldn't have an idea in his silly head. . . . My gentleman has condescended to give me children. Now he goes about making love to women who don't have children . . . or if they do, kill them for the sake of their precious figures. My gentleman loves the fine arts—the theatre —that is the theatre which he finds in some wretched hole of a café chantant . . . where he can drink with a lot of low women with faces daubed with paint— creatures I wouldn't touch with a pair of tongs. . . . It's more than likely that one fine day, he'll come home and poison his children, the brainless sot. . . . But for me he would have pawned everything we have long ago—to the shirts on our backs. An atheist who refuses to kneel down or cross himself before the blessed

Sacrament. He's as stupid as he can be, but that doesn't prevent him from talking philosophy—a lot of nonsense about liberty, the duties of a citizen, and so on. Liberty! Liberty to make a beast of himself. I'll liberty you, you wretch. . . .

M2. Yes, that is the real she—the real heroine! That is the creature whom I dare not leave for the sake of the divine being who intoxicates me like a magic potion, who provides the only reason for my still wishing to exist in this dreadful world!

(*As he says this he summons up the first concept of the singer. She sings and dances a can-can, gradually driving into a dark corner L. the second concept of the wife. Then she herself has to retreat before the first concept of the wife, who advances, a menacing but imposing figure, noble in sorrow.*)

1ST CONCEPT OF THE WIFE. (*To the singer.*) Go! I implore you to go. You have no right here.

M1. None. . . . She speaks the truth.

1ST CONCEPT OF THE WIFE. Since you do not love him, since you would not make the smallest sacrifice for him . . . since you have had many others in your life like him . . . leave him alone, leave him in peace, if you still have any heart, any decency. I need him— I need his support—his affection. Oh, don't take him from me—Don't tear him away from his family to whom he owes——

1ST CONCEPT OF SINGER. (*Interrupting mockingly and laughing.*) I know all those phrases by heart. I've heard them so often. They mean nothing.

1ST CONCEPT OF THE WIFE. Go away, do you hear? Don't drive me too far——

1st Concept of Singer. So now you're going to threaten me, are you? Why, may I ask? Why do you hate me? Is it because I have beautiful legs and firm breasts, or because my words fly like birds and leap like champagne corks?

M2. (*Applauding.*) Bravo! Bravo!

1st Concept of the Wife. What do you want but his money, you creature for sale——

1st Concept of Singer. What's that? A creature for sale, am I? What are you then? Didn't you sell yourself when you married him? Take it back—take it back, I say, or I'll——

(*She advances threateningly on the first concept of the wife.*)

1st Concept of the Wife. You shall go—Yes, you *shall* go!

(*They close with one another, and fight. The anguished heart palpitates noisily during their struggle. Violent curses and frenzied threats are heard, such as " You shameless wretch! " " You beast! " " You're only a harlot! " " I'll teach you! " " You bloody church-goer! " After vanishing from view for a moment in the dark corner L. they reappear more bitter and violent than ever now as the second concepts. The wife has the singer's transformation between her teeth. After a second change of personality, they reappear on the scene. The victory is with the singer, who is seen with the prostrate wife under her knee. The wife disengages herself, and, weeping, escapes L., followed by the laughter of the singer and the bravos of M2. Then M1, indignant, boxes the singer's ears, who runs to the back of the scene uttering plaintive howls like a whipped cur. M2, losing all control, throws himself on M1, and strangles him. The heart stops for a minute. Two or three nerves touched during the struggle snap. M2, seeing that his adversary is dead, throws himself at the feet of the singer.)*

M2. Come, my queen, come. My beloved, now you are mine, mine in everything, mine for ever, oh, my life, my joy, my love! . . . Come to me.

THE SINGER. (*1st Concept.*) No, you dear little silly. Oh, no! It has only been a joke. Money first . . . love afterwards. And from what I see— there's a sight more love here than money. . . . And how are you going to get any? No—no, *no!* I am not for you, my boy. It was all a joke.

(She disappears L.)

(M2 stands thunderstruck in a despairing attitude. A café concert air, of an exciting, irritating type, is heard in the distance. The first concept of the wife is seen. She fixes her large sorrowful eyes on M2. It is difficult to see whether she is nursing her sick child, or making reproachful signs to M2.)

M2. *(Madly hurling himself at the telephone.)* Quick! Quick now. It's all over. There is nothing. . . . I have come to the end of everything. . . . With what strength I have left I implore you to do it quickly. The revolver is in the right-hand pocket. Quickly, oh, more quickly! It will not hurt, believe me, not much. . . . Fire between the fourth and fifth rib. . . . What? You are afraid? There is nothing to be afraid of. It will be all over in a moment. Quick. . . .

(*There is a short pause, during which* M3 *wakes up abruptly and throws an uneasy glance round him. A loud report like a cannon shot is heard. The sound echoes through the vault of the soul. A great hole opens in the diaphragm from which pour out ribbons of blood. Darkness half hides the scene.* M2 *struggling convulsively falls under the heart drowned in the streamers of red ribbon. The heart has stopped beating. The lung has ceased to respire. A pause.* M3 *trembles and stretches himself wearily. A Porter carrying a lighted lantern enters.*)

THE PORTER. This is Everyone's Town. You have to get out here, sir. You change here.

M3. Thank you, yes. I have to change here.

(*He puts on his hat, takes his bag, and follows* THE PORTER, *yawning.*)

CURTAIN.

Milton Keynes UK
Ingram Content Group UK Ltd.
UKHW040001060124
435497UK00003B/91